Kaizen for Small Business

How to Gain and Maintain a Competitive Edge by Applying the Japanese Philosophy of Kaizen to Your Small Business

by Kato Nelson

Table of Contents

Introduction

The philosophy of *Kaizen* is thought to be responsible for Japan's incredible industrial rise from the ruin of World War II to one of the world's most vibrant, productive, profitable, and cutting-edge economies. Westerners began taking a serious look at *Kaizen* in the 1980s after the Japanese tech and automotive sectors established themselves as indomitable market players. Today, many well-known American companies, such as Boeing, rely on *Kaizen* principles in running their business.

Kaizen at its core is a type of business culture, one with an emphasis on tenacious and ceaseless forward momentum. Applying the philosophy of *Kaizen* to your small business can lead to wondrous improvements in employee morale, efficiency, and profitability. But in order to capitalize on the best *Kaizen* has to offer, you'll have to show some tenacity of your own as you institute a massive cultural shift in your workplace.

A Japanese word that translates to "improvement," *Kaizen* relies on heightened, vocal, and ubiquitous employee awareness within all levels of an organization. Team members are trained to continually seek out and report opportunities for

1

process improvement. This ongoing process of observing, reporting, and implementing is firmly and permanently ingrained into business operations. Identifying process improvement becomes just as ordinary and quotidian as punching one's time card.

If you're serious about taking advantage of these powerful techniques in your small business, then read on. This book will walk you through the essentials of implementing *Kaizen* processes, method-by-method and principle-by-principle.

Chapter 1: The Concept of Radical Teamwork

The 1st Key Principle of Kaizen

Sure, the idea of teamwork gets floated around in business all the time. But in reality, western businesses, especially small businesses, permit and even encourage subtle emphasis on individualism. When you visit *Bob's Auto Repair* downtown, you feel better knowing that Bob himself is working on your car. When you go to the coffee shop, you prefer to have your favorite barista, Janet, make your caramel macchiato, because you know that she's capable of making it just the way you like it. What's wrong with this picture? Well, according to the first key principle of *Kaizen*, everything.

In *Kaizen*, "teamwork" means a whole lot more than getting up during your break to help a co-worker during a rush at your restaurant. Here's an example of *Kaizen's* "teamwork" principle in action. A woman, let's call her Jenny, has a personal tradition she shares with her sister—they go to get manicures together at a specific nail salon. They do this once every two weeks or so. Jenny always gets her nails done by Victoria, while her sister always gets her nails done by

Benjamin. Unfortunately, Jenny has had some trouble recently with her nails breaking shortly after her visit to the salon. This has happened twice and she's beginning to lose faith in Victoria's competence as a manicurist. Jenny's sister has had no such problem and is quite content with Benjamin's work. The next time Jenny and her sister visit the salon, Jenny asks if she can have her nails done by another stylist.

The salon owner is made aware of Jenny's request and inquires of her as to the reason. Once made aware of the problem, the owner investigates the processes followed by both Victoria and Benjamin in an effort to find a reason why Victoria's process may be problematic while Benjamin's is achieving the desired result. He notices that Victoria applies coats of adhesive to the nails she's working on using a dabbing, circular motion, while Benjamin first outlines the border of each nail with adhesive. He instructs Victoria and the entirety of the salon staff to always outline the border of the nail with adhesive. He then informs Jenny that the problem has been solved and the next time Jenny visits the salon with her sister, he sends her back to Victoria to get her nails done.

In *Kaizen,* the team exists as a whole unto itself. Every team member brings the same process-optimized and uniform value, so there is no need for any individual distinctions to be made. The perfect *Kaizen* nail salon wouldn't even have regular pairings of specific manicurists preferred by specific customers. The entire staff would follow optimal processes and would understand the specific preferences and needs of every customer serviced by the salon. Now that's teamwork on a whole new level.

Of course, depending on the scope of your business, how many customers you service, and the degree to which customer expectations are customized, the perfect *Kaizen* team may be outside the realm of practicality for some businesses. Nonetheless, perfect seamlessness within the organization remains the ideal, and is continually pursued in the *Kaizen* business model.

The principle reason for such rigorous de-individualization of personnel is, of course, efficiency. If Jenny and other patrons can depend on Victoria, Benjamin, and multiple other manicurists to do her nails properly, then there's a cumulative decrease in the amount of wait-time. More customers are serviced over time, which means more profit for the business. The same efficiency boost can be realized if more baristas, rather than just Janet, can be trusted to make your caramel macchiato, and more mechanics, rather than just bob, can be trusted to work on your automobile. *Kaizen's* emphasis on a radical brand of teamwork is the first in a multitude of small incremental process improvements that together have the power to create remarkably successful businesses.

Chapter 2: Getting Your Employees on Board

The 2nd Key Principle of Kaizen

In terms of implementation sequence, this 2nd key principle of *Kaizen* should probably be addressed first. When bringing the principles of *Kaizen* to your small business, you absolutely, 100%, must have your employees on board. The number 1 pitfall for *Kaizen* implementation is a resistance to change, which is unfortunately all too common in American businesses. For a lot of small businesses, *Kaizen* will represent a distinct departure from business as usual, and as such is not always well-received by current staff members, especially those who've been a part of the organization for a long time and feel entitled to continue to do things the way they've always been done.

Kaizen makes leaders of all employees, from the shipping clerks to the executive vice presidents. Even the most manual of laborers become enthusiastically valued for their intelligence and creativity. Thinking becomes a part of their job. As great as this sounds in theory, it doesn't always go so smoothly in practice. Contributions are not just welcome under *Kaizen*, but expected. When process improvements are identified, it is likewise *expected* that all employees will adopt these improvements. And, when *Kaizen* is in full swing, these process improvements get rolled out on a continual basis, which some employees may find tedious.

In order for *Kaizen* to be effective, employees must embrace their unique worth within the organization. But they must also not allow themselves to become discouraged if their ideas aren't adopted by company leadership. In its purest form, *Kaizen* assumes an environment where employees feel supported by, and support, the company; they share their ideas freely, regularly, and enthusiastically, but defer to the judgment of senior leadership.

Given Japan's culture of collective identify and generally high education levels, it's not surprising that the *Kaizen* philosophy fits in well within Japanese culture. When exporting this philosophy to a small business in the United States, you're going to come up against some significant challenges. That said, if you're creative and persistent, you'll end up with a highly profitable and exemplary small business with high growth potential. Here are some ways in which you can encourage your employees to adopt *Kaizen:*

Use Seminars and Hand-outs—Introduce Your Employees to Kaizen Philosophy

You can hire an outside consultant, a *Kaizen* expert, to come in and introduce your employees to *Kaizen* via seminars. You should alert your employees to the fact that this is the direction in which you've decided to take the company. You may even warn them at this time that *Kaizen* is not going to sit well with certain employees and may even result in some of them parting ways with the company. Seeing as successful adoption of *Kaizen* will lead to an increase in profit, this is a good time to bump up the pay rate for lower wageworkers. This adjustment however, *must* come with a clear understanding on the workers' part that much more is to be expected of them from here on out. Their increased pay is a sign of their increased value to the company, as they are now responsible for the seeking out, sharing, and implementing of process improvements on a daily and ongoing basis.

Implement Improvements with a Clear Velocity

As a small business owner, *Kaizen* is not an excuse to embrace or even entertain every new idea that your employees think up. Let's be real. There are going to be some bad ones. As the leader of the business, your job is still to cultivate and follow a clear vision for the business' large-scale growth. By no means is *Kaizen* synonymous with leadership from the bottom up. It is instead a way by which more thorough engagement at the bottom levels may provide value to overall company functioning.

If Your Business Isn't a "Family" Business, It Is Now

You can't just stop with higher compensation for your employees. In order for your small business to flourish under *Kaizen,* you must create an environment in which your workers would be happy spending their entire careers. Your workers must be emotionally (or financially) vested in the success of the company. To do this, maybe you should consider moving to an employee-owned business model. You must ensure your employees have adequate medical care, that they get generous amounts of paid leave. Employees should work in good working conditions and should have ample opportunities to earn bonuses.

For team-building purposes, try to organize at least one team activity every two months (if not more frequently). Get a group of employees together to form a team for a softball or kickball league. Go out

16

for a round of paint ball, or you could always go with the basic company picnic. Make sure you have a Christmas party and at least one other holiday function during the course of the year. All in all, you need your employees to feel secure in their job, like they truly belong and are contributing significant value to the team. High employee morale is the lifeblood of *Kaizen*.

Chapter 3: Confident Sharing of Ideas

The 3rd Key Principle of Kaizen

Employees should always feel confident sharing their ideas. A good idea generated by a worker is much more valuable than an idea generated by a boss. Why? Because if the worker is the one who came up with the idea, he'll be more likely to work hard in order to ensure the idea's success. The *Kaizen* philosophy maximizes the opportunities for workers to contribute meaningful ideas to improve company processes. Furthermore, employees are more likely to feel valued when their suggestions are implemented by the company. When morale goes up, so does the likelihood that one of your employees will come up with a great idea to share. It's a perpetual, uplifting cycle. Here are a few ways to keep the fresh ideas coming in:

Open Door Policy

If you don't have one already, then you should implement a formal "Open Door" policy at your business, complete with a form for all employees to sign in acknowledgment of the policy. An Open Door policy is a guarantee that any employee may contact and request time with any member of management to discuss company-related issues. The Open Door policy supports *Kaizen* by encouraging more interaction between workers and management.

Team Meetings

Frequent team meetings, complete with a meeting agenda, secretary and presiding officers, provide a great forum for idea exchange at multiple levels. A specific meeting model, the "quality circle," will be explained in Chapter 5.

Suggestion Cards or Surveys

Even if you have a medium-sized business with 50 or more employees, you can still take advantage of simple feedback and suggestion cards or surveys. If you have someone on your team proficient in Microsoft Excel, then you can ask her to create a spreadsheet containing all of the data received during the survey. This data can be compiled and organized by keywords such as "expansion," "product improvement," "shipping and receiving," etc. Having all of your feedback organized in this way will allow you to pick and choose the areas where you want to focus. It's also nice to know that if 20 members of your team suggest the same general improvement, and you end up implementing it, all 20 team members will have their morale boosted thanks to your actions.

Chapter 4: The Never-Ending Path of Improvement

The 4th Key Principle of Kaizen

Firmly internalizing the 4th principal of Kaizen is critical if you're to have lasting success with this philosophy. What tends to happen during failed implementations of *Kaizen* is that the workers in a company, suddenly encouraged to voice their opinions, let it all out, everything that's been on their minds, and wait hopefully for massive change on an unreasonable timeline. This idealism lasts, of course, for about two weeks, and then everyone goes back to their normal routines and gives up on the new system, communication is, again, limited, a stark divide reasserts itself between the company's management and its wage-earners, and no lasting change is accomplished. Careful, thoughtful and tenacious adoption to the 4th principle ensures that what you accomplish with *Kaizen* will create lasting positive change.

The 4th principle of *Kaizen* is the principle of there always being room for more improvement. In other words, *Kaizen* is as much for ineffective companies in need of a full makeover as it is for wildly profitable companies at the apex of success. The principle is the same—there are always ways to improve.

Employees must understand that *Kaizen* is not meant to be a method by which a company takes stock of everything it's doing sub-optimally, constructs an action plan, and sprints its way through comprehensive renovations. *Kaizen* is an action plan of continuous action plans, a marathon rather than a sprint. What's more important is that the company institutionalizes a system of constant self-checking and process improvement. Furthermore, all employees must come to understand that finding opportunities for improvement is now a part of their most basic job detail. If they're not always improving, then they're not doing their jobs. Employees should be afraid *not* to speak up.

The way you structurally implement your feedback channels depends on the type of small business you run. If you run a service business, for example, like a restaurant, coffee shop, or bar, then one idea you might consider is to have a regimented 20 minute period each week where every employee fills out a questionnaire about their observations over the previous week, their thoughts on their own job detail and the overall functioning of the company. You should also, as the business owner, set aside some time to meet with the employees to discuss their questionnaires. Rather than prioritize the employees who are firmly engaged in the *Kaizen* process, focus on the employees who aren't returning meaningful feedback and don't seem to understand that this type of analysis is now as much a part of their job detail as pouring drinks for their customers. It's not something you can just skip if you don't feel like doing it.

You may discover during the course of these meetings that, unfortunately, you have some employees who just don't care about *Kaizen* or the general improvement of your business. They may be onboard just to get a paycheck and the level of intellectual and emotional commitment required by *Kaizen* may be more than they're willing to give. It may be time to part ways with these employees if you're serious about maximizing your success with *Kaizen*.

When hiring new employees, you should discuss *Kaizen* in the interview process and evaluate employees on the basis of how well they'd fit into the *Kaizen* culture. The best employees for *Kaizen* are those who have a history of innovation and process improvement and also those who are looking to make a long-term commitment to your business. Ask interviewees to give examples of instances in which they've made their jobs easier. Call references and past employers and see if you can get an idea of how committed the employee was at her previous job.

When properly nurtured, the ethos of continual improvement can produce amazing value for your small business. It can induce healthy competition among employees and even innovative approaches to service and product development.

Chapter 5: Establishing the Quality Circle

The 5th Key Principle of Kaizen

The use of the "quality circle" is another major principle of Kaizen. The first recorded use of this facility is attributed to the Nippon Wireless and Telegraph Company in 1962. This powerful concept quickly caught the attention of other businesses and by the end of the year, 36 other companies were using quality circles. By the late 1970s an estimated 1 million circles were in action with an estimated 10 million total employees participating. The popularity of quality circles soared throughout the 80s, and then died down some over the ensuing decades, despite being businesses which practice *Kaizen*. Large international companies, such as United Parcel Service (UPS), use quality circles to monitor occupational health and wellness issues.

A quality circle is a group of employees who regularly meet on company time to discuss process-related issues. Usually the employees who participate in the quality group work in the same or similar work environments and are familiar with the same challenges. Though the quality circle is an idea generating and problem-solving group, manual laborers are often an integral component. Quality circles are usually reinforced with highly trained personnel who know how to identify practical courses of action to address the concerns brought up in the group.

Quality circles are continuous and unending, they document and act on a steady stream of issues. Companies like UPS use a formal log to keep track of issues being handled by the quality circle. After each meeting of the quality circle members, items on the log are revised, expanded, or marked complete and key members of the circle (usually a manager and someone who represents the workers) must sign off on the log. This log is then periodically audited by higher-level management, thereby ensuring that the concerns reported and ideas for process improvement are communicated throughout all levels of the organization.

Quality circles are intended not only as a source of problem solving and innovation, but also as a morale booster. At UPS, for instance, all members of the quality circle are recognized with special attire and food is provided at each meeting.

Quality circles should be implemented with enthusiastic and visible support from management. If the management does not care about the proceedings of the quality circle, it will quickly become a waste of time for all participants. Managers can use quality circles to put them in touch with the on-the-ground realities of the business and the concerns and ideas of its employees. Workers can benefit by experiencing first-hand the value of a robust exchange of ideas. Whenever possible and when aligned with company interests, management should take action on items identified in the quality circle.

Even though quality circles are more traditionally associated with larger organizations, small businesses can also take advantage of this powerful tool. In a small business setting with five to 20 or so employees, a quality circle will be composed with as few as four employees (though there isn't really an exact minimum. The key concern is that the members of the circle share the same working environment and represent a diverse array of formal responsibilities. Since participation in a quality circle is traditionally paid time, it may get a little expensive for a small business owner to conduct weekly meetings. Bi-weekly or monthly meetings are ok.

Chapter 6: The Five "S" Framework of Kaizen

The 5S framework is used in Kaizen to emphasize business organization practices that are conducive to the continuous improvement practice implicit in the system. In this chapter we'll take a look at the five "S"s and how they can be used to improve your small business' work environments.

Seiri

The first "S" is for "Seiri"—translated to "sort" in English—and is meant essentially to dissuade against a cluttered work environment in order to maximize efficiency. In following the principle of Seiri, there is no room for items crowding the work environment without purpose. For instance, consider the grocery chain "Trader Joe's." If you take a look at the frozen isle and other select areas of the Trader Joe's supermarket you'll notice that many of the products are fit into boxes of similar or identical size. The reason for this is that Trader Joe's does not want to stock an item unless it's going to sell in respectable quantities. This is an especially critical consideration for Trader Joe's, because they are working with much less floor space than a traditional supermarket. If the product doesn't sell, then the product must not be allowed to take up any precious room, no exceptions. If an item doesn't sell according to expectation, then Trader Joe's will simply stop making the product and create a new product in the exact same size box, pouch, or jar to displace the product which is not selling. The result is less labor spent on removing overstock, more sales, and much more revenue.

For a smaller business, you may not have the amenities available to constantly churn out new products at the drop of a hat, but that doesn't mean that you can't powerfully utilize to your advantage the Seiri principle. Start by doing a good 80/20 analysis of your workspace. An 80/20 analysis is based upon the idea that about 20% of the products in your inventory are purchased by customers 80% of the time, while the remaining 80% are purchased 20% of the time. Start digging into that 80%, taking away products that don't sell well and replacing them with new products. Don't allow random miscellanea to park itself indefinitely in your workspace without pulling its weight. The 80/20 principle can be used, not only to analyze your saleable inventory, but also to analyze almost any other work-area resource that you keep on hand. Start by taking a simple look at your cleaning cabinet. Which 20% of your cleaning tools and products do you use 80% of the time? Can you get rid of anything that's not doing much other than getting in the way? Take a look at your desk and filing area.

You can probably part ways with receipts from 1975. And finally, before moving on from our discussion of the 80/20 principle, you have to take a hard look at your staff members. Do 20% of your staff members do 80% of the work? Is there a way to acknowledge your outstanding performers and improve or dismiss those who are just along for the ride?

Killing the clutter in your work area will allow you to relax, work more efficiently, and if you regularly maintain and prune your work area with bonsai-worthy precision, you will over time inevitably realize an increase in profitability in your small business.

Seiton

The second "S" stands for "Seiton," which in English translates to "Set in Order." Seiton is about eliminating motion for motion's sake. Have you ever worked with (or for) someone who felt they had to always run around like a mad man in order to feel productive, when, in actuality, they accomplished very little? This is an example of a person who's not "Set in Order."

The Seiton principle applies not only to personal restlessness but to material restlessness as well. After the Seiri phase is accomplished and you've cut out all the clutter and noise, then it's time to concentrate on implementing sensible organization schemes for the stuff you're holding onto. You can exercise Seiton by making sure that everything you have in your work environment is placed somewhere that makes sense and maximizes functionality and efficiency.

The goal of the Seiton phase is to minimize movement in your workspace and ensure that the movement that does transpire is as low stress as possible. To analyze movement in your workspace, you can use a spaghetti diagram to visualize the various movement paths in your workspace. Do this by creating a simple sketch of the workspace, then use threads to indicate movement paths. If you like you can use different colors to denote varying concentrations of traffic. This type of analysis can be helpful for warehouses, restaurants, factories, and other work environments that depend on the expedient movement of goods and personnel.

Another method is to use post it notes and a bulletin board. Use the post it notes to create a flow chart that illustrates the basic movement processes of the work area. Together with your team, you can evaluate these movements, deciding whether or not they are absolutely necessary or whether there's a way to accomplish the same projects using fewer steps, perhaps by rearranging objects in the room or stationing personnel in different areas. These subtle changes may seem only small tweaks, but *Kaizen*, as a philosophy, is built around the importance of several small, but intelligent improvements that create significant cumulative effect. And given the amount of time spent engaged in one's work surroundings, eliminating a few feet of unnecessary movement here and there will have a profound effect over time.

Seiso

The third "S" in the *Kaizen* framework for good housekeeping is "Seiso", which, in English, translates into "Shine." It's always nice to start your workday in a clean environment, but the Seiso principle, however, is about much more than just sanitation. The true purpose of Seiso is to create an environment where irregularities stand out. For example, if you've got a pipe that's leaking, it will be much easier to see if the pipe isn't already engulfed in dark dirt and debris from months of neglect. Seiso holds that every corner of the work area should be left spic and span on a daily basis and that equipment should be repainted regularly to look "like-new." Keeping a disciplined cleaning regimen will allow for problems to be easily recognized and addressed when they crop up.

When implementing Seiso in your small business, instruct your employees to both clean *and* inspect the items in their work area. Your Seiso time is not for mindless scrubbing and wiping, but for thoughtful examination of the overall health of your work area and equipment.

Seiketsu

The "Seiketsu" principle translates to "standardize." This step involves institutionalizing the first three "S"s intelligently and exporting them to other areas of the company. For a small business, your principle concern is with the former directive, institutionalizing the first three "S"s. Seiketsu is where you guarantee that all the work and money you've invested in *Kaizen* doesn't fizzle out and go to waste but remains a permanent part of your business process. In order to ensure these processes remain whole and healthy, you will need to make sure that the time and resources needed to regularly complete your new routines are always available.

To accomplish Seiketsu in your small business you can use a daily checklist or introduce a Standard Operating Procedure to incorporate regular cleaning and decluttering activities. You reserve times, once or twice a week, to monitor your employees at the end of the day and make sure they are taking the time they need to implement the first three "S"s.

Shitsuke

The fifth and final "S" is "Shitsuke" which translates to "sustain". For a small business, Shitsuke is about continually devoting resources towards the maintenance of *Kaizen* principles. One of the best ways to achieve Shitsuke is to invest in regular *Kaizen* training seminars that keep these powerful ideas fresh in your mind and in the minds of your employees.

Another important way to achieve Shitsuke is by following your own advice. You should be following the five "S"s and the other *Kaizen* principles in your own work area. Your employees will notice this and will understand that this isn't something you're doing just to keep them on their toes (although it is in a way) but it's also something you truly believe is helpful to the wellbeing of the company and its employees.

Finally, the use of audits are helpful in ensuring that the new 5S Framework is sustained. 5S audits can be used as a part of the employee evaluation process. A few best practices for 5S audits:

- Scoring is best kept numeric and non-subjective. Using a scale of 1 to 10 to evaluate the cleanliness of the serving counter with 1 being poor and 10 being exceptionally clean is preferable to having employees write in descriptions.

- 5S audits should be conducted by a disinterested third party, someone who works outside of the work area being assessed, or even by you, the business owner.

- During the initial stages of 5S implementation, audits should be conducted more frequently, 2 to 4 times a month. After the big initial changes have been made, then you can reduce the frequency of the audits at your discretion.

- For incentives, you can offer awards for the shift or work area that scores the highest on the 5S audit—coupons, gift cards, or company paraphernalia, etc.

Remember, the name of the game in *Kaizen* is <u>continuous</u> improvement. Let nothing grow stagnant, even the processes you use to monitor compliance with 5S should be continually assessed and improved.

Conclusion

Hopefully this book has inspired you to give *Kaizen* a try in your small business. If you've decided to take the plunge, then it's best that you fill your employees in on your grand plans as soon as possible. There are going to be a lot of changes and some of them will inevitably be met with resistance. That's to be expected.

When executed well, *Kaizen,* installs a remarkable sense of company ownership in your employees. Employees who make a strong connection with the five "S"s and other principles will feel vested in the well-functioning of their work areas and will be a fount of creative and useful ideas that they themselves will execute. And as a small business owner, it simply doesn't get any better.

Finally, I'd like to thank you for purchasing this book! If you enjoyed it or found it helpful, I'd greatly appreciate it if you'd take a moment to leave a review on Amazon. Thank you!

Made in United States
Troutdale, OR
09/16/2023

12960930R00029